Silver Burdett Picture Histories

World War I

Pierre Miquel
Illustrated by Jacques Poirier

Library of Congress Cataloging in Publication Data

Miquel, Pierre, 1930-
  World War I.

  (Silver Burdett picture histories)
  Translation of: Au temps de la grande guerre.
  Summary: Examines World War I, its beginning, its
effect on the countries involved, life in the trenches, the major battles and incidents, and the
aftermath of the war.
  1. World War, 1914–1918—Juvenile literature. [1. World War, 1914—1918] I. Poirer,
Jacques, ill. II. Title. III. Title: World War One. IV. Title: World War 1. V. Series.
F522.7.M4813   1985   940.3   85-40207
ISBN 0-382-06889-0

Translated and adapted by Charlotte M. Kossmann
from *La vie privée des hommes: Au temps de la grande guerre.*

First published in France in 1984 by
Librarie Hachette, Paris.

Adapted and published in the United States in 1985 by
Silver Burdett Company, Morristown, N.J.

Contents

1914–1918
The First World War

The Great War, which began in August, 1914, and finally ended in November, 1918, was one of the most important events in the history of the world.

A VERY SAD APPRAISAL

When the war began in August, 1914, no one believed that it would last much longer than a few weeks or months. It was going to be "short and sweet." No one imagined that nine million men would die gassed, machine gunned, or shelled (France alone lost 1,310,000), nor that 6,500,000 soldiers would live the rest of their lives as invalids. This was the first total war in history. Sixty-five million men were mobilized, almost all of the world's nations were involved, and vast portions of the European continent, from the Atlantic Ocean to the Ural Mountains were devastated as a result.

August 4, 1914 young Germans leaving for war

European nations engaged the populations of their colonies in the war. Soldiers were called upon to form "imperial" armies. New Zealanders, Canadians, South Africans, and Australians, as well as Indians and Egyptians, fought in the British army. Two hundred thousand soldiers came from Morocco, Algeria, Senegal, and Indochina to serve in the French army. The Turks enlisted Arabs, Lebanese, and Syrians in their forces. The first American troops

A group of mobilized troops in Paris

to debark and fight in France were black Americans from Harlem or Virginia. German war propaganda tried to rouse the Moslems against the colonial powers, while British propaganda awakened Arab nationalism against the Turks. Arousing the colonized people was one result of the war. In many territories the native populations asked, in the name of the war effort, for an end to the colonial system and a move toward freedom, if not total independence.

French and American
infantrymen on a battlefield

AN ECONOMIC AND FINANCIAL DISASTER FOR EUROPE

In addition to the loss of human life, the damage to property was also significant. The large scale destruction which occurred in the combat zones of France hastened the decline of the countryside. For several years after the war, millions of acres remained unsuitable for cultivation. Many towns, virtually leveled by bombing, had to be completely reconstructed after the war. In the north and the east of France, it took ten years for mines and industry to recuperate and return to prewar production levels.

By 1918 all of Europe lay in ruins. Great Britain and France had to repay the loans they had received for national defense, in addition to the massive amount of help they got from American private capital. Germany and Austria-Hungary were bankrupt. Their currency had no value and their economies were sorely lacking capital. As for Russia, since 1917 the country had also been engaged in a revolution. The European powers saw the Russian financial and economic markets closed forever. In addition, from this time on the Bolshevik form and international concept of revolution would threaten Central and Western Europe. All of Europe had entered into a period of war and revolution.

World War I was more beneficial to the newer countries outside of Europe which didn't suffer directly from the conflict — the United States of America in particular. Indeed, since 1917, our country had sent two million soldiers to the Old World. At the same time, Americans realized there were considerable profits to be made in financing the European war and by selling massive amounts of wheat, cotton, horses, arms, and chemical products. Canada and Australia, meanwhile, were also industrializing at the same rate. In the Far East, Japan took advantage of the elimination of the Germans from the China Sea to start its own expansion.

The town hall in Arras
after the bombing

WHY WAR?

But how did world affairs reach this point, and why did the war begin so easily in Europe? The industrial powers found themselves in competition, but their interests weren't necessarily in opposition. They were in agreement on dividing the world and pulling profits from it, even at the cost of unfair exploitation. Britain assumed the role of a lion, Germany and Italy were virtually excluded. Russia was an open target for Western capitalism. It hadn't sufficiently developed its own industrialization and was still a huge, rural nation, where millions of peasants lived miserably in overpopulated villages. Bonded servitude had been done away with just fifty years earlier. As for Austria-Hungary and the Ottoman Empire, they barely had the means to control the different ethnic groups within their borders who were demanding independence. These old empires had trouble retaining their cohesion. They were vulnerable to the slightest upheaval.

"Death to world imperialism" —
A Bolshevik propaganda poster

German infantrymen in action

TWO BLOCKS
CONFRONT EACH OTHER

Their only protection was to ally themselves with other nations. Austria-Hungary was united with Germany through a political and military treaty which guaranteed total cooperation in the event of war. Italy was also a part of this treaty which formed the "Triple Alliance," but was an unreliable partner at best. Not only did Italy refuse to join their side when the war began in August, 1914, but actually went on to enter the conflict on the side of the Allies. It is true that the Germans, to make up for the Italian defection, found a more important ally, the Turks. Constructors of the famous Bagdad railroad, the Germans had strengthened their position in Turkey considerably by bringing in about 5,000 "specialists" with Liman von Sanders.

Elsewhere in Europe the "Triple Entente" united France with Great Britain and Russia. Indeed, since 1904, all colonial competition had been forgotten, and an *Entente Cordiale* was established by Great Britain and France. These two countries had signed a military agreement and France had persuaded Great Britain to get closer to Russia. A type of balance, therefore, developed in Europe — two antagonistic groups confronted each other—the Triple Entente and the Triple Alliance. Despite their continual conflicts, the small Balkan nations didn't seem to be able to disrupt this balance. Consequently, in July, 1914, no one in Europe thought much about the dangers of war.

Nevertheless, the Old World was truly a powder-keg. "Scientific" novelties and a surplus of fearsome weapons had been accumulated in the arsenals.

The British and German navies were in competition with each other. Giant battleships called *dreadnoughts* were a formidable means of destruction. Their anchors alone weighed ten tons. In the face of accelerated construction by the German Admiral Tirpitz, Britain risked losing the supremacy of its navy.

AN INEVITABLE WAR?

To defend the area that they had taken from France in 1871, Germany had built fortifications in the area around Metz and on the Alsatian plain. The *Meuse-line* was impregnable and directly threatened the French border above Nancy. Artillery weapons had made rapid progress. Krupp in Germany, Schneider in France, Putlivoc in Russia, and Skoda in Czechoslovakia were the leading arms manufacturers of the time. They competed ferociously for markets in the Balkan nations to sell their rapid firing cannons, whose shells were usually charged with a new explosive called melinite. The new arms, the French 75 mm. cannon and the German 77, could release a downpour of fire power on infantry lines, making war even more murderous. Military units were also heavily equipped with Maxim and Hotchkiss machine guns. These guns were also mounted on the German *Taube* airplanes, which were used to bomb and raid villages behind the lines, just as the zeppelins, that were difficult to see at night, were used.

Russian (on the right) and
French soldiers getting supplies.

A British artillery gun

After a tense political debate in 1913, to confront the German threats, France had extended the duration of military service and brought the number of recruits in the regular army up to 750,000 men. Wilhelm II in 1913 had declared that he believed the war to be "unavoidable and necessary." All the countries of Europe prepared themselves for it, but no one believed it would be all that serious.

The Germans and the French had sold weapons to the Greeks, the Bulgarians, the Serbians, and the Turks. But they didn't believe that a general armed conflict would occur since these small Balkan nations periodically tore each other apart. Nevertheless, it was because of the small kingdom of Serbia that Europe entered into war and mobilized twelve million men on the battlefields in the first hot months of the summer of 1914.

WAR BREAKS OUT

On June 28, the Austrian archduke, Franz Ferdinand, was assassinated by a Serbian nationalist in Sarajevo. He and his wife had been on an official trip to Bosnia, an Austrian-Hungarian province. Vienna accused Serbia, which was protected by Russia. On July 29, the Czar ordered his troops to mobilize on the Russian-Austrian frontier.

All of Europe grew concerned. Afraid of surprise attacks, every country, as of July 21, prepared for war. By August 4, even Great Britain had declared war on Germany. They sent an expeditionary force of 150,000 men to France because the neutral country of Belgium had been invaded by Germany. In a few days, trains had transported millions of troops to the frontier. The Great War, that would later be called World War I, had begun.

For four years, following the Battle of the Marne, ten French departments were occupied by the German army, and torn up by a system of trenches that stretched for almost 300 miles from Flanders to Switzerland. The war moved into Central Europe. In 1915, Italy rejoined the Western side and fought against the Austrians in the Alps. The Serbians had to abandon their country in the face of the Austrian-German offensive, which was supported by Bulgaria's entry into the war. After their defeat at the Dardanelles, the Allies created a front at Salonika, blocking the German-Bulgarians from any access to the Mediterranean.

In Eastern Europe, the Germans and the Austrians came up against an inexhaustible Russian army which they just barely managed to stop at Western Prussia and push back beyond Poland. The Russians succeeded in creating a continuous front from the Baltic to the Black Sea to hold back the upsurge of the Turks in the south, who were unable to invade the Caucasus. Thus, the war became complete and worldwide.

In the Near East, the Turks tried to seize Suez and threatened the Persian Gulf forcing the British to raise a large army in India, and to encourage the raising of Arab contingents to hold back the Turks at all costs. The participation of colonies and dominions, and especially the United States entry into the war in 1917, brought all the continents into the conflict. Thus, the whole world took part in the spectacular suicide of old Europe.

A 75 millimeter cannon being loaded

7

A 1915 French government
poster asking for gold loans to support the war effort.

PRINCIPAL MILITARY FORCES IN AUGUST, 1914		
	ALLIED POWERS **(France, Russia, and Great Britain)**	**CENTRAL POWERS** **(Germany and Austria-Hungary)**
POPULATION	253 million	115 million
ARMED FORCES	FRANCE 93 divisions GREAT BRITAIN 5 divisions RUSSIA 99 divisions + 42 cav. div.	GERMANY 94 divisions AUSTRIA-HUNGARY 49 divisions
WEAPONS	FRANCE 308 cannons 2,200 machine guns	GERMANY 548 cannons 2,450 machine guns
AVIATION	FRANCE 150 planes GREAT BRITAIN 66 planes	GERMANY 174 planes
NAVAL FORCES	GREAT BRITAIN 64 battleships 121 cruisers FRANCE 28 battleships, 34 cruisers 73 submarines	GERMANY 40 battleships, 57 cruisers 23 submarines AUSTRIA 16 battleships, 12 cruisers

Leaving for War

In August, 1914, troops were mobilized and men left for war during harvest time. Anxious European peasant families were sorry to see these able-bodied young men leave the fields for draft centers. Yet strong feelings of patriotism were evident everywhere. In Great Britain, where obligatory military service didn't exist, volunteers were recruited by the millions. Even neutral countries, like Switzerland, which weren't part of the conflict, mobilized and equipped fortifications along their German and French borders.

All the European countries that were involved in the conflict were convinced that they should fight for their rights. The Russians were going to fight to help the Serbians, their brothers in race and religion. The Germans were mobilized because of the Russian threat; the Cossacks were just a few stops away from Berlin. The British hurried to come to the rescue of invaded Belgium. As for the French, they left for war with two purposes in mind, to protect their country against invasion and to win back Alsace-Lorraine from the Germans.

The mobilized believed that the war would be short. In Germany, they gave themselves six weeks to enter Paris. In France, the generals hadn't foreseen that winter uniforms would be needed by their troops. The French soldiers were only provided with cloth caps, not helmets. In the first bloody battles of the war they died by the thousands from head injuries. Military headquarters didn't believe in manufacturing helmets. They were that convinced of a quick victory over the Germans.

When, by the end of 1914, everyone realized that the war would be long, patriotism quickly changed into chauvinism and governmental propaganda became fierce. Governments organized censorship of the press and mail, so that public opinion would support the war effort. It was also proving to be an expensive war. Soon, many countries found themselves persuading their citizens to lend them gold for national defense. All these war loans would be repaid, but investors would be ruined.

State loans financed the war. In every country, banks organized poster campaigns to drain off savings.

paganda raged even in the neutral countries. The Germans, who imported large quantities of food products and textiles from ...in, organized a war museum in Barcelona where they illus...ed their victories and the superiority of their newest arms.

The recruitment of volunteers in London's Trafalgar Square. Thousands of young people enlisted in Kitchner's K divisions. The British sent just 150,000 men to the European continent at the beginning of the war. Three years later the number was 2,500,000.

..e war will be short: at the most two or three months," said the ..n who were mobilized in both Paris and Berlin. The recruits left ...ng with recalled soldiers in units commanded by active and re-..ve officers. Crowds rushed to the train stations to see them off.

..the beginning of September, 1914, General Gallieni, military ...vernor of Paris ordered the city's taxis to transport 4,000 men ...the battlefield of the Marne in the north. The taxis, cheered on ..the crowds, made several trips loaded with soldiers.

In Berlin the enthusiasm was indescribable. The soldiers were covered with flowers, the Sisters of Charity passed out tea and coffee. The men left saying they would be home by Christmas. The same enthusiasm could be found in Paris.

During the days of mobilization, German-owned stores and those suspected of being German stores, were ransacked in Paris. Many Swiss and Alsatians were mistaken for Germans and arrested. People denounced groups of foreigners, threatening to harm them.

Empires and Democracies at War

The governments that brought their countries into the war were constantly watchful that the war effort was supported with the greatest vigor. With the exception of Great Britain, the legislatures had not even been consulted before war was declared.

In the empires of Central and Eastern Europe, the military ruled without mercy, imposing their decisions on everyone. Because his generals were rather inept, Czar Nicholas II, autocrat of all Russia, took it upon himself to direct the war. At last, he found in Broussilov, Alekseev, and Youdenitch, competent and energetic generals who could take on not only the Turkish and Austrian armies, but even the Germans. They extracted an enormous war effort from the civilian population without even consulting them or asking them their opinion. In Germany, the military, led by Moltke, and then Falkenhayn and Hindenburg, dictated political decisions to the Chancellor, who did not have the power to oppose them. The military in Austria was also all-powerful.

The Western democracies involved in the war also depended heavily on the generals who commanded their armies. But the hesitations of political leaders, the influence of public opinion, and the instability of the government ministers in 1916 and 1917 gave an impression of wavering. Two energetic men served as examples of saviors and governed without weakness. In Great Britain, Lloyd George, the Welshman, and in France, Clemenceau from the Vendee, convinced their legislatures and the public that the war should be pursued to the end. But when the United States entered the war in 1917 they were forced to contend with the ideas of President Wilson, who wanted a "peace without conquest or annexations." Socialists in the European countries rallied around this concept of peace, but their governments did not.

In 1914 at *Tsarkoie Selo*, the Czar's summer palace, Raymond Poincaré, President of the French Republic inspected the Russian army on parade. The army was large and well equipped with Schneider cannons. The Russian alliance was vital to France. It alone was responsible for keeping the German divisions from rushing to the west.

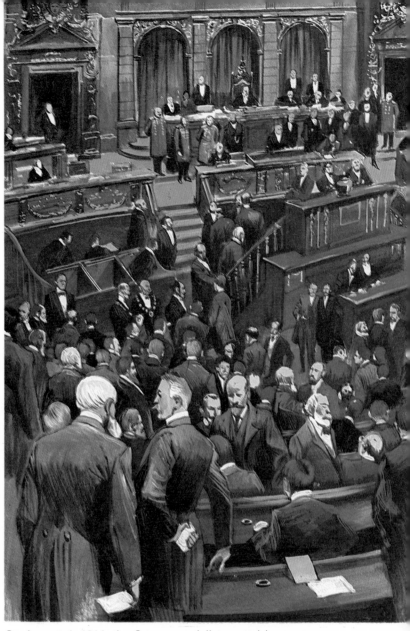

1918, President Wilson of the United States, arrived in Brest, [to] make peace in Europe. He was greeted by warm socialist [de]monstrations. His conception of peace without penalties, or [ter]ritorial conquest was well received by all the European leftist [pa]rties.

[Kai]ser Wilhelm II, and his son the crown prince of Prussia, fre[qu]ently inspected the troops at the front. The Kaiser's visits to [Fra]nce were numerous. He went there for all the big battles, [par]ticularly to Verdun, where the prince was in charge of [op]erations.

[De]spite his advanced age, Clemenceau frequently visited the [tre]nches and grew more popular among the French soldiers [wh]o loved his battered hat and his legendary mustache. They [call]ed him "The Tiger."

On August 4, 1914, the German socialists voted by an over-whelming majority, to give the Reichstag military power. France's socialists also rallied to support the war, in spite of pacifist orders from the socialist international in July, 1914.

King George V of Great Britain often crossed the Channel with his son, the Prince of Wales, to inspect their troops. The troops were cheered by his appearance and greeted him in the British manner with hurrahs.

Working for the War Effort

In all the European countries, work for the war effort was tremendous. German industry had to produce 500,000 shells per day, and supply 350 new cannons every month. Three million tons of steel were needed to manufacture ammunition. The Germans mobilized their 40,000 miles of railways and priority was given to transporting war matériel. For four years engines steamed back and forth, bringing equipment, ammunition, and men to the French, Russian, and Balkan fronts and even to the Near East.

France's war effort was just as formidable. At the beginning of the war, the German army's advance deprived France of its supply of coal from the north. As a result the areas of Firminy, Saint Etienne, and Le Creusot became vital. War industries concentrated production in these place as well as in the Parisian region. Because of the lack of iron from Lorraine, they exploited the small iron mines in Normandy, in the center of France, and in the Pyrenees mountains. In all the French towns, traditional industries were converted so they could produce much needed grenades and helmets.

With the help of its navy, Britain was able to obtain supplies from France and later from Italy. The Allies had 4,000 vessels at their disposal. They were going to suffer from submarine attacks and many ended up at the bottoms of the oceans. The British navy also had to take many risks in the North Sea to supply Russia with much needed arms and ammunition. Naval shipyards worked at full speed to replace the merchant marine vessels that were destroyed and to win the battle of supplies which was essential to winning the war.

A special effort prepared the French ports to receive British and then American aid. The railroad companies then brought the supplies directly to the front.

Coming out of the oven, this cannon is tempered in a vat of oil. In Germany, Krupp made the heaviest artillery pieces. Some 420 mm cannons could project shells 1.40 meters long, weighing 800 to 900 kilos.

14

roads played an important role in the development of the war. [o]n the first day of mobilization, France used 3,600 locomotives [and] 150,000 box cars. The Germans had a powerful railway system [whi]ch allowed their troops great mobility. There was soon a lack of locomotives to pull heavy freight trains. The engines were repaired so that they would last a little longer. The Germans were obliged to buy freight cars from Switzerland at outrageous prices.

[tru]cks became more and more numerous on the roads leading to [the] front. Large castings of rubber were taken from the factories [to m]ake the solid tires that were used on the artillery carriages and [truc]ks at Verdun.

[In t]he port of London, the shaft and crankshaft of a large vessel [are] transported on a barge. During 1917, the British fleet suffered [con]siderable damage at sea. They had to repair ships non-stop [whi]ch had been damaged by submarine torpedoes, as well as

The automobile assembly line was created in the American factory. Here a Model T Ford is being assembled. Thanks to this process, vehicles needed by the Allied armies during the war were manufactured in the United States at a fast pace and sent to France.

build new ones. In England the steel mills forged huge naval guns which were to be mounted on the giant battleships, the super-dreadnoughts—23,500 tons of steel, armed with twelve 305 mm. cannons.

Women's Work: From Field to Factory

Everywhere in Europe the war split apart families, mobilizing several dozen million young and active men, most of them from peasant families. In the countryside, women, assisted by children and the elderly, managed to carry on the farm work. Helped by prisoners of war or soldiers of the national guard (the army reserve which was composed of older soldiers), the women gathered in the harvest, took care of the livestock, and drove the machines.

In the steel mills women turned the shells to make them perfectly round and smooth. Standing in front of lathes all day, the jets of oil made the task particularly difficult. In the chemical factories acid turned the workers' skin yellow from time to time. Yet none of these tiresome, unpleasant, or even dangerous jobs discouraged them. A day of work in a factory lasted ten to thirteen hours, sometimes even fourteen hours. Many crews worked through the night and sometimes even on Sundays.

In all the countries involved in the war, the women played a decisive part in the battle to step-up production. In France, in 1917, women took over the offices and workshops alike when 5,200,000 men were called upon to defend the flag. Known as "munitionnettes," 430,000 of them worked in arms factories. They earned one-third the money that men did and had to strike to win equal pay for themselves. In 1916, in Paris, out of a total of 300,000 factory workers only 60,000 were women. Just two years later, there would be almost 100,000 of them.

The women workers quickly proved that they could replace men very well in several trades — as checkers, blacksmiths, calibraters, and makers of pontoons. In some firms, women were in the majority, at one factory they numbered more than sixty out of every hundred. Soon, bosses and unions grew to depend on this new supply of female labor.

16

Workers at their posts in the foundries of Saint-Chamond in the Loire Valley

stern Prussia, near the Russian border, and throughout the
of Europe, the peasant women had to plow the land them-
s. The village and the neighboring farms were deserted by
en who had gone off to war.

pporetto in 1917, the Austrians broke through the Italian lines.
e rear, panic was felt throughout the province of Venice.
en were requisitioned to dig trenches in the villages and to
p strong lines of defense.

ns of shoes were needed by the famous French infantrymen
d poilus. Women worked in workshops stitching leggings. The
er was bought in Argentina or in North America. They also
p vast numbers of workshops to resole salvaged shoes.

In the Berlin train station, the station master was a woman. Civilians had no space on trains. Only musicians and invalids could put
their instruments or their chairs in the baggage cars. The high price
of train fares discouraged civilians from traveling.

The town-criers, who shouted the news and bulletins were also
called to war. Therefore women had to replace them. The Postal
Service even engaged women to deliver the mail. In May, 1917,
Paris saw its first postwoman.

Civilian Life

In all the countries involved in the war new workshops, both large and small, were set up to produce supplies for the armies. Factory production grew increasingly efficient. On the assembly lines the workers kept working harder and harder to produce more and more. At the same time, high prices, a lack of merchandise, and many, many restrictions made life very difficult for civilians. During the last three winters of the worldwide conflict, the shortage of coal in particular was sorely felt.

The populations of the countries at war all suffered differently from the lack of food. In France as well as in Britain, aid arrived by sea. The Americans sent wheat, corn, and barley and also delivered flocks of animals. Cereal, fruit, and wine were provided by North Africa, Spain, and Egypt. Because of the Allied blockade there was a lack of provisions in Germany and Austria. Food was rationed to the people there.

To survive, families ate food substitutes, such as ersatz sugar and artificial fats. The food shortages also affected their health. In 1917, fifty out of one hundred children had growth problems due to inadequate diets. About 500,000 of them were sent out of the cities to the country or even to neutral countries for a period of one to three months. A type of scurvy was discovered in Berlin. Cases of typhus fever were found in towns in the south of Germany. Deaths due to tuberculosis were on the increase. Gripped by panic, and fearing for their lives, many people believed they had returned to a period similar to that of the black plague. To avoid contamination and spread of diseases, schools and colleges were forced to close their doors.

Parisians line up in "Vilgrain sheds," installed on the sidewalks by a minister of Clemenceau. To fight against the high cost of living necessities were sold here at reasonable prices. Clemenceau wanted to lower the increase in retail prices.

mbs were manufactured in workshops which were sometimes
te small. Bomb heads were reheated in the forge before being
t into place. Aviators often hurled their bombs by hand, since
ir planes were not equipped with devices to release them.

Under the supervision of a reservist, miles of barbed wire were
loaded at Vierzon. Sabotage on the railroad lines in Belgium and
Northern France occurred frequently. The railroads were also carefully watched over to spot spies and escaped prisoners.

ctors were overwhelmed by the number of victims of the Span-
flu epidemic. They searched for new ways to disinfect homes.
nobile sterilizers like this one, linens that had come into contact
h the sick were soaked in formalin.

Russian factories built tractors to make plowing faster and more
efficient in the rich, black-earth plains of the Ukraine, the wheat
granary of the Czar's empire. But there simply weren't enough
tractors.

erican factories were reorganized to speed up the production
niforms. In workshops like the one pictured here workers out-
d and cut up to 380 tunics at once. They had to quickly put

two million American soldiers, who were being shipped to France,
into uniforms.

Soldiers from Five Continents

Soldiers came from all over the world to fight in this war. Starting in 1917, two million American "Yankees" were sent overseas to join the Allied lines. Among the first sent were four regiments of blacks from Harlem and Virginia. The Polish in America enlisted soldiers from among their native-born sons. The Canadians came to the aid of the British and died by the thousands on Vimy Ridge.

Senegalese and Moroccans came from Africa and formed the sharpshooter cores in the French regiments. The Zouaves enlisted along with whites from North Africa, and the Turcos (Algerian Zouaves) joined with the natives. From Morocco came the turbaned Spahi calvarymen. Africans died at Dixmude, beside the marines, while the Turcos were killed at Charleroi. From South Africa other units came and the famous Anzacs came from Australia and New Zealand. The British recruited a large number of Indians into their army in the Near East.

As early as 1914, the Garibaldians, Italian volunteers, began going to France to fight. Russian brigades were sent to the West to engage in the fighting. Employed as shock troops, the Russians were very effective on the offensive. The Russians mobilized Czechoslovakian prisoners and Poles out of the Austrian army. Serbians who escaped from the long retreat reenlisted to fight with the Greek Venizelos army on the Salonika front. French generals in the East commanded units made up of British, Italian, Serbian, Greek, Russian, and African soldiers, as well as several units from France itself. They enlisted Indians, Madagascans, Tunisians, and Indo-Chinese as auxiliary troops. At Salonika nearly every language imaginable was spoken. The Turkish army was equally diverse with its German instructors, its infantrymen from Anatolia, and its Arab, Syrian, and Lebanese units. In 1918, almost all the races of the world could be found in the trenches.

Scots parade through a demolished town in northern France. The shrill bag pipe music uplifted the hearts of civilians living in their cellars.

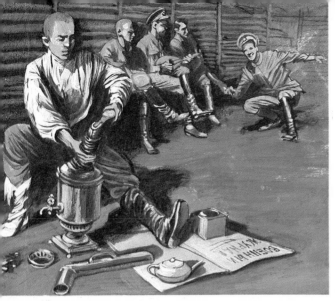

...g his boot as a fan a Russian soldier lights up a samovar. ...h his comrades will be able to drink hot tea. Notice the peaked-... they wore. Like the French at the beginning of the war, Rus-...s didn't have any helmets to wear.

In Italy during the campaign in the Dolomites the Italians desperately lacked artillery and ammunition. However, they were able to protect their border at the Alps by using the resources of the environment.

...he Allied front, Indians shivered from the cold. Military leaders ...ld have prohibited the use of these troops in Europe. They ...n't accustomed to the cold climate. They should have been ...d in the Near East where the temperatures were warmer.

These Turkish artillery men, trained by the Germans, are using a Krupp cannon. The view-finder (at the right) came from Leipzig. They wore helmets without visors, for their religion did not allow them to shade their eyes from the sun.

...ne camp at Mailly in France the canteen had an international ...osphere. At the bar, you could meet Americans with their large ...hats, Italians or Portuguese with their peaked-caps, and, of ...rse, French and British soldiers. Despite the fact that they all

spoke different languages, the soldiers mingled easily. They were subjected to the same ordeals in battle and shared the same daily life on the front lines between offensives.

The War Becomes Entrenched

On September 10, 1914, after the battle of the Marne, the Germans withdrew to an entrenched position all along the Aisne front from Soissons to the Rheims mountains. The French tried to follow them but they ran out of shells for their cannons and horseshoes for their horses. When they attacked at the Aisne, the German army was well prepared with a solid system of trenches reinforced by cannons and machine-guns in blockhouses. The French offensive was stopped short. To protect themselves, the French troops also dug trenches. But both adversaries, in an effort to outflank the other, quickly sent units toward the northwest. It was still a war of movement, witnessed by this "race to the sea."

Nevertheless this wild race finished in bloody battles in Belgium and at the North Sea. Neither army could gain a decisive advantage. The intensity of the fighting, at all costs, forced the soldiers to take cover by digging in and building fortifications.

Thus, the war became entrenched on a 450-mile front, from the North Sea to the Vosges. A second continuous line of trenches, separated by an area less than a mile wide and called "no man's land" was being created. Day after day each line of reinforced trenches blocked the two equally strong forces from breaking their enemy's line. Hundreds of thousands of lives were sacrificed for insignificant ground gains. The war was changing into a long war of attrition, a war of trenches, resulting in the slow destruction of the enemy by nonstop shelling. The war would go on for three and a half years, until the spring of 1918.

From February to July, 1916, there was only one access road over which supplies could be brought to the front at Verdun. Under continuous bombardment, crews worked full time to keep it in passable condition. Captain Doumenc's trucks traveled both night and day, bringing in supplies, and taking out the wounded and soldiers who had leave.

the Russian front, German artillerymen were equipped with trajectory field mortars, the fearsome *Minewerfers*. These apons were easily moved, and covered, and made infantry at-

tacks easier. The French came up with a similar weapon called the trench mortar, which fired blade torpedoes. On the left a soldier uses a periscope to observe the enemy without being seen.

ese soldiers are preparing to throw hand grenades at enemy sitions to flush out the machine-gun nests located under con- te gun turrets. They had to crawl up to within a few yards of openings and quickly throw in their grenades.

ese soldiers are installing a portable telephone line. It has to be ted before they put it up. The telephone allowed artillery ob- vers to transmit information to their battery chiefs. It was vitally ded.

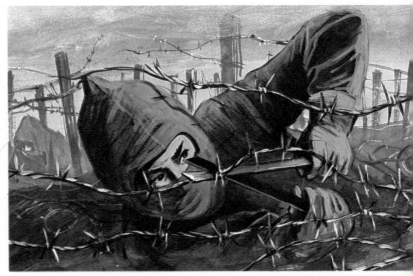

At dawn, sappers would crawl up to the network of a barbed wire that protected the enemy's trenches. They would cut the rows of barbed wire with heavy shears to make gaps that would allow shock troops to break through more quickly when they attacked.

Artillery bombardment destroyed all the telephone lines. The outposts often sent and received their orders and information by carrier pigeons. In the foreground is an "armored" cage to carry the pigeon and protect it from shell fragments and stray bullets.

The Men in the Trenches

Night and day, the men in the trenches constantly kept watch on the front and faced attacks from the enemy. Mostly, it was a question of localized attacks to correct a position, or to gain a foothold in a more advantageous spot. These battles, which took place frequently on certain fronts, like the Éparges or Bois-le Prêtre, resulted from the military staff's determination to equally fortify their lines eliminating any weak spots. The men, who felt that they would be dying for nothing, generally hated these deadly skirmishes.

General offensives were feared even more. Preceded by long and violent artillery bombardment at the beginning of the war, and by more localized but intense bombardment at its end, the battles were fought at Verdun, on the Somme, in Flanders, in Artois, and at Chemin-des-Dames. Veterans say that before the German offensive at Verdun, in February, 1916, the men were so deafened and worn out by the shellings, they were on the verge of falling asleep while standing in the trenches with guns in their hands. When the shock troops attacked with fixed bayonets, the soldiers in the lead faced the brunt of the cross fire from the machine guns and the mortars' explosions.

Until 1917, leaves in the French army were rare and infrequent. Any rest the men did get was too close to the firing line for them to really regain their strength. The men at the front felt that those in the rear had forgotten them, and that they didn't realize the extent of the soldiers' sacrifices. They demonstrated their hatred for civilian ''goldbricks'' and ''shirkers'' who remained at home. They also complained about certain duties (inspections, ceremonial parades, drills during rest periods), and the praises and congratulations given them by deputies and ministers, whom they scorned. The war was long and cruel. As it dragged on the soldiers in the trenches often wondered if it would ever end.

The marines at Dixmude were transported in armored trains to save the Belgians who were retreating from the Germans. They set up entrenched positions to block the enemy's push forward. The soldiers stumbled in the wet and icy mud. The parapet, slotted with holes for firing, provided the soldiers with protection from enemy bullets.

...diers placed explosives in tunnels dug under enemy lines. This ...per examines the rockshaft walls with a doctor's stethoscope ...order to detect the exact position of the German trench.

In the Artois, British soldiers built wooden shelters which were covered with a thick layer of mud. These soldiers play dominos while smoking their pipes. Other soldiers were up in the trenches watching the enemy.

...cross section of advanced positions. A. A shelter for mortars, ...apouillots or Minenwerfer). B. Protected shelter for riflemen. C. ...volving gun turrets for the machine gunners. D. Rest shelter. E. ...nch trenches and their outposts. 1. Undermining shaft tunnel ...the dirt which is removed in baskets. 2. Shaft communication

trench where they put the explosives. 3. Lookouts stationed at outposts. 4. A German countersap mine. 5. An engineer digging a hole for dynamite in order to block the enemy tunnel. 6. A wall of explosive being prepared at the end of the communication trench.

...is lookout is being relieved. He has spent several hours on a pile ...earth looking out of a peephole. In the foreground is an alarm ...rd that would be pulled in case of danger. The lookout is in a ...ry isolated outpost, and even if he is tired he musn't sleep.

Looking for a pail of water, these French soldiers have gotten lost in the German lines. They will now become prisoners. But how could they find their way out of this intricate network of communication trenches, when positions would be taken and retaken?

New Weapons for Combat

For four years, the European war became more and more industrialized. The casualties, the deterioration of equipment, and the continual increase in the need for army supplies required the warring nations to continue to develop and improve their methods of production.

The armies lined up their guns by the thousands on the battlefields. Projectiles were counted by tens of millions. One barrage, which covered a front that stretched for just over a mile in length and was half a mile deep, used twenty million shells. At Verdun, in one day, the Germans shot off 800,000 shells.

New weapons were developed and quickly appeared on the battlefields. The Krupp arms factory, in Germany, produced heavy howitzers, capable of projecting shells at targets several dozens of miles away. These German guns could also destroy concrete blockhouse fortresses like those found in Liege and Namur. The French supplied not only the Serbians and the Russians with Schneider matériel, but also the Americans who used the 75mm and the 155 mm rapid-firing cannons.

The largest pieces of artillery were loaded onto flat cars and transported by rail. After 1917, they were mounted on machines with very large caterpillar tracks. This made it much easier to move them around and gave them greater manueverability.

In France, Peugeot and Renault produced the first armored car. However, they were not capable of going everywhere—steep slopes, deep ditches, and barbed wire slowed them down or blocked their routes. For this reason the British developed the first tanks under the strictest secrecy. Near the end of 1916, they first appeared on the battlefield. But these early tanks moved slowly and were very vulnerable. In 1917, the French invented the small armored Renault tanks, about twenty feet long and six feet wide. These new vehicles accompanied the infantry and took out the machine-gun nests and hidden field batteries. They could shoot an average of fifteen to twenty shells and five to six hundred cartridges a minute.

On September 1, 1916, German soldiers quickly abandoned their posts when the first tanks arrived at their lines. These early tanks might have looked quite fearsome, but could only move at a speed of four miles per hour.

ctober, 1917, on the Chemin-des-Dames plateau in northern ce, a Zouave battalion reached the ruins of Fort Malmaison, ch was held by the Germans, and took the position. The attack preceded by an intense artillery bombardment, and the use

he beginning of the war, the French artillery units were pped with nearly 4,000 75 mm guns. These guns were very ctive for stopping any infantry advancements; but they were ually useless against the heavy German guns.

of tanks and airplanes. The attacking troops used flame-throwers. These deadly weapons allowed them to reach the machine-gunners holed up in blockhouses, which were inaccessible to the bombing.

The British also had heavy artillery. These guns, which they called "Long Toms", allowed them to mount counterattacks against the German guns. These officers have decided to camouflage their artillery gun, to prevent it from being seen by enemy observers.

e Germans brought heavy guns up to the front lines. Then they ed the way for the offensives by launching powerful artillery rages into enemy trenches. Here, a Howitzer 210 is set up in a tery. The firing will be directed from the observation post nes-d in the tree (on the far left).

A War of Terrorism

When an artillery bombardment was finished, silence fell over the front. Suddenly the section officers blew their whistles, and bugle calls gave the signal—charge!! The infantry jumped out of their trenches, scared to death, and advanced on the enemy lines to overpower them and take their trenches, at any cost. The soldiers carried shovels to put the enemy trenches back into shape after the battle. Tens of thousands of troops fell in these advances.

Even if land battles couldn't be won with the help of modern technology, the techniques of war could be improved to bring death to and triumph over the opponent. The Germans were able to improve some methods which they had copied from their opponents. With their new weapons, they were able to break through and destroy an enemy front. Advances in rapid-firing artillery allowed them, with specially trained attack troops, to develop the famous ''rolling-fire'' of artillery which preceded the infantry's advances. It neatly cleared everything in the infantry's path. The attacks had to be synchronized, for if they weren't the artillery fired on their own troops.

In April, 1915, on the Western front in the area of Ypres, the Germans conducted an attack preceded by poisonous gas for the first time in the war. When the strange, heavy, greenish-yellow cloud, carried by a gust of wind, hit the French-Canadian trenches, it was a total surprise to the Allied infantrymen. They attempted to protect themselves as best they could against this fatal cloud by placing wet handkerchiefs in front of their faces. Things had taken a new turn, terrorism was now part of the war.

As the months went by the Germans used the toxic, suffocating gases with more and more frequency. Shells charged with the fearsome mustard gas were systematically fired on the Allied lines. The military was now forced to equip the soldiers with gas masks. They also tried to protect the dogs and the 600,000 horses of the French army by supplying them with protective bags, which allowed them to breath without harm.

German infantrymen leaving their trenches with fixed bayonets

28

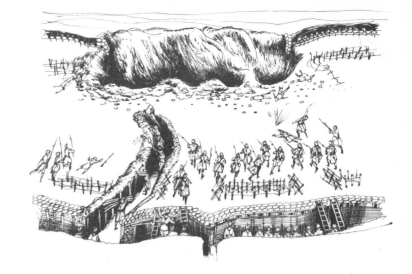

An infantry attack against an enemy trench had to be accompanied immediately with a fierce effort by diggers to build a communication trench. This allowed easy access into the conquered trench and protected the soldiers from artillery and machine gunners.

ht attacks were launched under the light from flares. They sur-
ed the sleeping soldiers who were overcome by gas shells
ch exploded on top of the blockhouses. They were forced to
 in the cold and the mud until reinforcements arrived.

e a position had been won, isolated machine-gun nests needed
e destroyed, and the survivors terrorized so that they surren-
ed easily. In the French army Senegalese soldiers inflicted a
ible panic among the German infantry.

These machine gunners are Portuguese armed by the British. Two divisions fought for many months on the Western front. They were called "Serrenos." The British commanders, who always lacked manpower, appreciated these brave and strong soldiers.

On the Isonzo front, Italian Arditi, equipped with breast-plates and maces fought with false arms. They are reminiscent of medieval knights. They fought with blanks in the Austrian trenches. The Arditi finally removed the Austrians by sheer force.

Life at the Front

On the front, soldiers led a precarious life. They improvised to find ways to fight against the cold, mud, body lice and other parasites, and the many invisible enemies that they had to guard against to live properly. They arranged their huts and rear line shelters as best they could. When the soldiers weren't at the front, they camped in ruined villages just behind the lines, where they didn't always have a roof to sleep under. They had to wait until 1917 before they were finally issued bedding. Up until that time they slept on straw, awakened occasionally by long-range guns. Whenever possible the mail-carrier brought mail, newspapers, and other news from home to the trenches. The soldiers waited impatiently for him. Those who weren't married sometimes had "war godmothers" in the rear who wrote to them regularly.

Clothes wore out quickly. Pants didn't last longer than three months, coats lasted about six months, and jackets ten months. Charity organizations also sent packages and warm articles (especially wool socks) to the soldiers. Meanwhile, the trenches were more or less outfitted. Very often, as in the Champagne caves, the Germans were even able to install hot water and central heating. The British used showers at Artois. The French and Italian positions were often poorly outfitted. The men complained of the cold and the mud, and frequently they found themselves up to their knees in it. The soldiers in the West ate better, even though the Germans had given priority to the army's food supplies. The French soldiers did not experience any shortage of wine or fresh vegetables, although they found themselves eating cold soup all too often.

Kitchens on wheels, like this one, served soldiers just behind the lines (in 1917, there were 6,000 of them in the French army). The men were provided with hot soup, vegetables, and coffee. They read military newspapers like *Le Canard Enchaîné*, or letters from home while others peeled potatoes.

30

keep themselves busy during the calm periods, the French sol-
ders made objects that they sold in the rear. Some used aluminium
m shell fuses to chisel out rings. Others sculpted little clay stat-
s of "Jerrys" (Germans). They also made canes, oil lamps, and

s German soldier knows how to use a sewing machine. They
 him "mother of the regiment," because he is always in demand
 his pals. In the background, another is typesetting a newspaper
 t will be read in the trenches.

of course, pipes. Tobacco helped the men keep a grip on themselves. During the first two years of war, twenty-two million packages of tobacco were given out officially.

The luxury of having a shower was provided here thanks to an
ingenious device set up on a creek in the Argonne forest. These
men are also taking advantage of the water to wash their clothes.
Body cleanliness was mandatory, to avoid fleas and lice.

ile a British mail-carrier (baggage-master) delivers the mail
m London, a soldier takes a souvenir picture of some dead rats.
ey were captured along thirty yards of trench, within just a half
 hour. Every dead rodent's tail earned the hunter a prize.

The Maimed

When a battle ended, the stretcher-bearers, directed by an auxiliary doctor, set out and tried to locate the wounded. Sometimes the wounded had to wait for hours for aid to come to them between the front lines. While waiting they stood the danger of being buried alive by mud tossed up by exploding shells.

First aid was administered on the spot. Then the wounded soldier would be carried on a stretcher to the nearest first-aid post, usually only a hundred yards away. From there, he would be taken by an ambulance stationed at the front to a field-hospital. Later, these survivors of major battles would be called *gueules cassées* (the maimed) by the French.

The field-hospitals lacked pharmaceutical supplies. Often the men were not even put to sleep before they were operated on. To care for 100,000 wounded, 100 tons of cotton, 50,000 quarts of peroxide water, 3,000 miles of bandages, 100,000 bottles of blood serum, and 70,000 casts for upper and lower limbs were needed. An extensive civilian aid movement was responsible for enlisting volunteer nurses.

The armies were constantly in need of soldiers. The convalescents didn't stay behind the lines in the rear for too long. As soon as they were fit they were quickly sent back to the front. Many soldiers were wounded more than once. Their "small wounds," which allowed them to leave the front and escape the threat of death for a while made them happy. During the early battles eighty out of one hundred French soldiers who were wounded had head injuries. They didn't have helmets and the metal crowns they put in their kepis (cloth caps) hardly protected them enough. They waited until September, 1915, before the French army supplied them with the *Bourguignotte*, a protective helmet made of sheet steel, which had been invented by a military quartermaster.

With the help of specially trained dogs, British stretcher-bearers look for the wounded between the lines. A column of men grope their way between the shell holes. They have been blinded, victims of mustard-gas. The man in the foreground received a shell fragment in the leg. He will be operated on in the field hospital.

...aplain says a few prayers over the body of a soldier who has ...died in a first-aid post. The wooden crosses as well as the ...ins are ready. A member of the local police force will reach his ...ily in a few days with the news of his death.

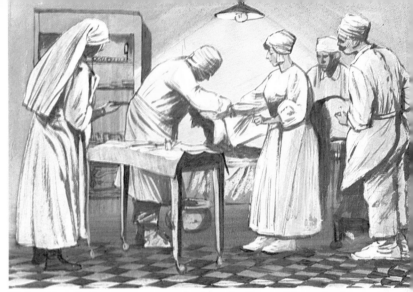

High society ladies set an example. Here is Queen Elizabeth of Belgium in the operating room of a surgical shelter. The wounded man is provided with an artificial limb—one more maimed person.

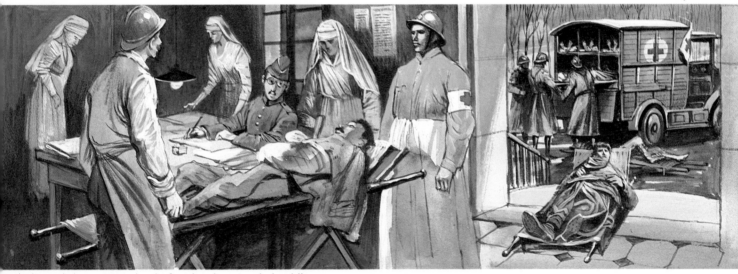

...ambulance brings a new load of seriously wounded soldiers ... field-hospital. The wounded have been left on the top steps, ...ause the stretcher bearers must leave right away for the front ...ind other soldiers. A large number of arm and leg wounds

...tles, churches, private homes, hotels, and large department ...es in Paris were transformed into hospitals. As a result of an ...eement, the wounded French soldiers who had been taken pris-...r received medical care from German doctors.

were recorded, as well as those who had been gassed and would never use their lungs or see again. Medical help had to be improvised. A long war had not been foreseen and the hospitals were filled to overflowing.

Officers here observe the rehabilitation of the seriously wounded. The officers organized gardening contests for men who had been fitted with artificial limbs. These men had to return to civilian life knowing how to use their artificial limbs.

Revolt and Fraternization Among Soldiers

During the long lulls between two offensives, soldiers from the opposing armies often met between the lines to talk, exchange tobacco or wine, and even in the case of some play a game of soccer. On Christmas Day, 1914, these spontaneous exchanges of fraternization were frequent, and the officers didn't dare stop them.

"Why are we fighting?" asked the infantrymen. Many of the sixty-five million men mobilized from one place or the other fought without knowing why. Even those who volunteered and left their homes with great enthusiasm, like the French, the Belgians, or the Germans, were beginning to ask questions. This started as early as 1914, when the soldiers came to the realization that the war was going to last much longer than had first been anticipated. When will it end? What good are all of these sacrifices? Why not stop this massacre? Didn't the pope ask for an armistice? These were thoughts that were going through many soldiers' minds. The fraternization movement was based on these feelings, and was at its peak at the end of the first year of war. The military leaders quickly put their armies back in order and goverments defined their war aims. Germany didn't want to evacuate and surrender Belgium or Alsace-Lorraine, so they were forced to continue. And the French soldiers had to put up with all of these sacrifices to see that this would be the war to end all wars.

In 1917, the soldiers on both sides were worn out. Many went on strike against the war. On the German side, desertion grew more frequent. In May and June there were serious mutinies on the French front, too. The military leaders severely punished the mutineers to make the men return to their posts, and keep them there. The leaders had to define the political reasons for the war. From then on the soldiers knew they had the right to leaves, to get occasional rest behind the lines, to have warm soup, and when they went home, to ride fast trains without waiting at the stations. But why had it been necessary to shoot men in your own army to reach this point?

These adversaries fraternize around the only water hole in the area.

34

...serters from the Austrian Army arrived by the thousands at the ...manian border. The deserters were Serbians, Poles, or Ruth-...ans, and they didn't want to fight in a war that wasn't theirs. ...e German officers, who commanded them, couldn't stop them.

...May, 1917, between Soissons and Anterive, the French infantry ...ew up the butts of their rifles, demanding that the fighting end. ...ny units were involved in the mutinies. Petain, who led the ...ression, quickly processed the sentences of those arrested.

The Russian revolution of 1917 didn't mean that the Czar's soldiers could abandon the front. Instead, they continued to fight bravely for the new republic. But when they found out that the Bolsheviks, who came to power in November were asking for peace, they fraternized with the Germans who gave them pamphlets.

Many of the soldiers who deserted were German. Besides Alsatians, Lorraines, Poles, and Danes, who were recruited into the German army by force, there were many Saxons who also deserted. They fled to the Dutch border, where they were very often arrested.

The War at Sea

One of the causes of World War I was naval armament. As a matter of national pride the British and the Germans had competed fiercely with each other to build up their navies. They constructed huge, armor-plated superdreadnoughts, weighing more than 30,000 tons. These naval monsters could fire several shells, weighing a ton each, per minute, and afterwards, with a speed of 21 knots, quickly pull away.

How could such expensive vessels be used in battle without running the risk of losing them? Admiral von Ingenohl, who commanded the German navy in 1914, didn't like taking these risks any more than his British counterpart, Admiral Jellicoe, who commanded the Grand Fleet.

The only battle during the whole war that the Admirals could provide, was the relatively indecisive battle of Jutland, which took place at the southern end of Norway. Along with naval actions at the Falkland Islands, it was the only important confrontation on the seas. On the night of May 31, 1916, Admiral Reinhard Scheer, commanding the German Fleet, believed it

possible to risk a sortie into the North Sea. A tremendous encounter took place, putting the whole British Grand Fleet against the German Fleet. Afterward, the British emerged as the winner of the battle.

As a countermeasure submarines became a new and fearsome weapon. The Germans, who knew how to use them, quickly became masters of the underwater seas. All the German submarines were designated with the letter U, followed by a number. The letter U is the first initial of the word *Unterseeboot* (submarine).

The shipyards had to make an enormous construction effort to build the convoys that supplied the Allied countries, and the warships to maintain the blockade of Germany and Austria-Hungary. The attacks of German submarines on neutral merchant marine, particularly the American ships, was the main reason why the United States entered the war in 1917.

The submarine war. A German submarine has just sunk a cargo ship in the Atlantic. The U-boat breaks the surface. In this case the submariners pick up the survivors.

rman submarines were a constant threat to the Allied fleet. The rchant ships were strangely camouflaged to fool the periscopes submarines which also sank passenger ships. Some cargo ships re armed with cannons and only moved in convoys, protected by patrols of cruisers and destroyers. Minefields were laid as defense and false boats used as traps to confuse the submarines and sink them.

1915, a U-9 German submarine, commanded by Weddigen, and wered by four very slow gasoline motors, succeeded in torpe-ng several British cruisers. This exploit was in turn publicized war propaganda. Weddigen could have an iron cross painted the conning tower of his vessel.

aval battle at night. The German armor-plated "Thuringen," rying 380 mm guns, each of which could fire a one ton shell minute, has sunk a British cruiser. When a shell fell vertically

In 1914, the Germans had only a dozen submarines at their disposal. When they realized the efficiency of this new weapon, they decided to build many more. These very uncomfortable vessels were also very easy to maneuver.

on the deck of the warship, it had attained a speed of 1800 mph. The range of the German guns was longer and more precise than those of the British.

Knights of the Sky

At the beginning of the war, the Allies, like the Germans and the Austrians, had only small airplanes. They were built with wood and canvas, and could only reach a speed of a mere sixty miles per hour. They were used only for reconnaissance and observation for the artillery. The pilots had a radio on board and relayed information back about enemy troop positions and their gunsites. As the war progressed, the military staffs had faster and more efficient planes built by the thousands.

They learned very quickly how to mount machine guns on the front of the airplanes and to synchronize their fire through the propellor's axle so it didn't damage the blades. A fighter force was soon born. The aviators who flew these planes fought fierce duels above the trenches, and the "aces of aces," Guynemer, Foncks, Madon, and Nungesser confronted von Richtofen and Goering.

Beginning with the battle of Verdun in 1916, fighter planes were used to machine-gun enemy columns and fire upon the infantry during attacks. Techniques for bombing from airplanes were also developed. The Germans were the first to perfect planes capable of dropping bombs on the villages in the rear. The British and the French, in their turn, built bombers which allowed them to attack submarine and Zeppelin bases. Zeppelins were giant dirigible airships which were capable of making flights of rather long distances.

The British built the first aircraft-carrier in history, designed to allow them to attack submarine bases. The French set up the first anti-aircraft gunsites to protect the civilian population against raids from the German airplanes called *Taubes*. In 1916, these airplanes scared people more than actually harmed them.

A dogfight. A German airplane, the Albatross, has just attacked and hit an observation "sausage." The airman in it has parachuted. A French Spad gives chase to the Albatross. The Albatross has a black iron cross on its wings; the Spad has a tricolor rosette.

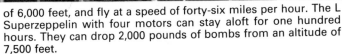

Zeppelin crew was the pride of Germany. This one is getting ly to drop bombs on the British. There are eighteen men in the partment: machine gunners, bombers, radio operators, and gators. The heavy tri-motored Z airship can climb to an altitude of 6,000 feet, and fly at a speed of forty-six miles per hour. The L Superzeppelin with four motors can stay aloft for one hundred hours. They can drop 2,000 pounds of bombs from an altitude of 7,500 feet.

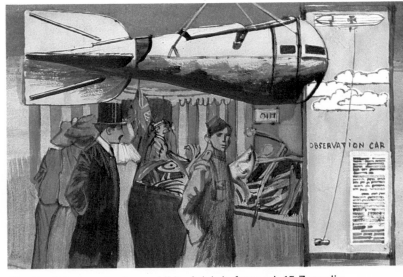

e French used machine guns and improvised anti-aircraft guns prevent enemy airplanes from flying over their lines. The ma- ne gunners here have mounted their weapon on a wheelbarrow eel. They rip the air with a shower of bullets.

ginning in 1916, instruments made by Voisin made night bomb- possible. Aviators dropped bombs by hand with great impre- ion. They spotted targets poorly and the winged explosives were t powerful enough to do much damage.

The English organized an exhibit of debris from a L-15 Zeppelin, which had been shot down at the mouth of the Thames in 1916. In the foreground is a nacelle. When a Zeppelin was lost in the clouds it would be lowered, with an observer on board, by a cable.

Firing through the propeller. 1- A steel angle (deflector) was at- tached to every blade in front of the gun to divert the bullet in case it hit the propeller. 2- Thanks to a rod operated by the motor, an improved system synchronized the gunfire with the propeller.

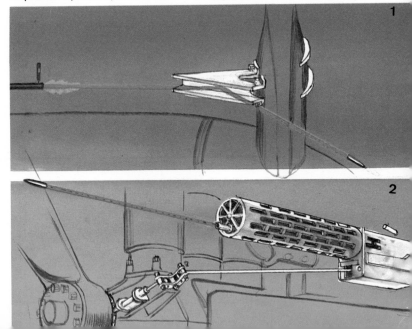

Displaced People

For four years, Belgium and northern France felt the effects of a very severe occupation by an enemy army that took away half of the civilians' food. Healthy men were taken for compulsory service, and women and children were evacuated to Switzerland and eventually repatriated to France. Thus, there were no unnecessary ''mouths to feed.''

The French government had to take in immigrants from all the other European countries. Belgian refugees populated Normandy, people from the northeast of France settled in the southern regions. Serbian refugees landed in Marseilles after their country had been invaded, as did Armenians who were escaping from the 1915 massacres. Lebanese and Syrians also came.

Soldiers from countries oppressed by the Austrian-Hungarian army surrendered by the hundreds of thousands to the Russians on the eastern front. In Russia, more than 1,300,000 prisoners were looking for ways to survive by working on farms. The Poles were also numerous in the West as well as in the East.

Prisoners were not treated the same by enemy countries. While the Germans had nothing to complain about in the British and French camps; the Russians in Germany were dying of hunger. However, in general, the threat of reprisals and the terms of the Geneva Convention encouraged each country to be very conscientious about the treatment of prisoners. Sometimes in Germany they were assigned to work in the mines. The French sent a certain number to Morocco and Algeria. The Germans tried to convince the Moslem prisoners from the French army to join the Turkish army. A small number were tempted. Many of them were captured again during the Palestine campaign, and reenlisted into the French army.

40

After the German invasion in August, 1914, entire Belgian families left their country. Most of them found refuge in France, but some went to England where public welfare organizations were slow to organize relief.

the prison camps the Germans feared epidemics of typhoid ~~fev~~er, small pox, tuberculosis, and syphilis. Therefore, they con~~du~~cted periodic disinfections of the barracks and the prisoners, ~~wh~~o, in some camps, also suffered from malnutrition. Daily rations

~~In~~ northern France, the German army seized all the available ag~~ric~~ultural food products, reducing the population's share to a very ~~m~~eager portion. The Germans organized evacuation of civilians in ~~th~~e occupied areas to eliminate unnecessary mouths to feed.

often consisted of a thin concoction called "soup" and a piece of turnip. War prisoners could not be employed in factories manufacturing war matériel, but nothing forbid using any available healthy sets of hands to work in the fields.

During December, 1915, the Serbians abandoned Serbia which had been invaded by the Austrians, the Germans, and the Bulgarians, and retreated through Albania to reach the Adriatic. Civilians followed the military, dying by the thousands from hunger and cold.

~~Aft~~er the Russian Revolution of February-March, 1917, the Austri~~an~~s and Germans grabbed the rich wheat fields of the Ukraine to ~~fee~~d people in the Central Powers who were starving as a result ~~of~~ the Allied blockade. The army harvested the crops themselves.

Suffering in the Cities

France and Belgium suffered terribly from the war, which had been fought for four years largely on their land. The ten occupied French departments comprised the major portion of the combat zones. Artillery from both sides destroyed the villages and towns all along the front. Rheims, a martyred city, suffered continuous bombing as did Soissons and Arras.

When the German army crushed Belgium, the people fled to escape the bombing, the reprisals, and executions of hostages. At Liege and Louvain, Namur and Brussels, the heavy artillery shells did not spare the cathedrals, the libraries, or the museums. Even outside the combat zones, systematic bombing of civilian targets had become routine. The terrorist war put everyone in the towns, women and children included, at the mercy of the artillery shells and the bombs dropped from airplanes and Zeppelins.

Toward the end of the war, in 1918, a long-range gun, called the Long Max, bombarded Paris every day along the north-south axis of the Strasbourg and St. Michel boulevards. In one day, on Good Friday, there were eighty victims. The Zeppelins terrorized the civilian population even more than the artillery. They conducted their murderous raids even in and around the city of London, provoking strong reactions of indignation.

When the war finally came to an end, the total damage to property was overwhelming. In France alone 289,000 houses were destroyed, 422,000 others were damaged, and more than six thousand acres of good farm land had been made unusable by the fighting. The cost of the damage totaled about 130 billion francs in gold.

A fire at the linen market of Ypres, a town that was heavily damaged by the fighting.

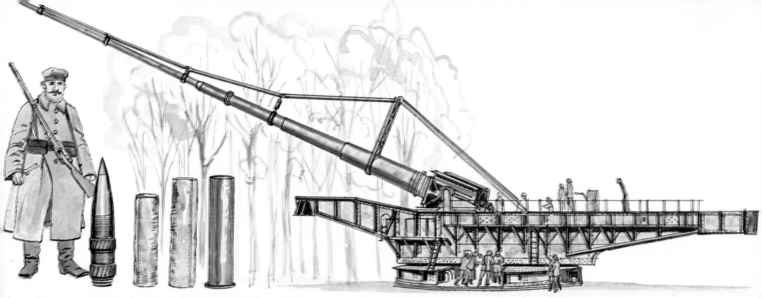

Long Max gun bombarded Paris, March 23, 1918, at 7:15 am the first time. The Parisians nicknamed it Big Bertha because y believed that it was the famous giant mobile German howitzer t measured 432 mm. but they were wrong. In reality, the Long

Max gun was even more impressive than the real Big Bertha. It weighed 142 tons, with a barrel length of nearly 385 feet and a medium range of 75 miles. Each barrel could only fire sixty times, and had to be replaced afterwards.

aris, in 1914, onlookers didn't rush to the shelters when German be airplanes appeared overhead. Were the Parisians who went into the streets to watch the maneuvers of these airplanes rudent or courageous?

bridge was destroyed by artillery fire. To cross the river, Bel-civilians had to appeal to ferry operators. The zone occupied he enemy was subjected to nonstop shelling by the Allies and abotage by specialized agents working undercover.

In this underground school in Champagne improvised classrooms were set up in cellars less than a mile from the front. The children followed their lessons with volunteer teachers without suffering any ill effects from the continuous bombing.

Due to shelling by German artillery the equestrian statue of Joan of Arc at Rheims was taken down from its pedestal by military engineers. Sand bags, to protect the cathedral's foundation, which had already been shelled several times, can be seen.

The Rebirth of Faith and Mysticism

The war encouraged a new devotion to religion all over Europe. Crowds of people sought comfort and hope in churches and temples. At the front, masses and group prayer services provided by the priests and pastors brought many soldiers closer together.

There were many units with their own priests. A total of 25,000 priests wore the uniform of the French army. Many were stretcher-bearers and picked up the dead and wounded between the lines. The Jesuit priest Teilhard de Chardin was a stretcher-bearer with the fourth Zouave regiment.

Moslem soldiers at the front practiced their religion and recited their prayers in the trenches, bowing to Mecca. The Russians marched off to war behind their icons and sang religious rather than patriotic songs. Orthodox priests were never far from the front lines and accompanied the dying in prayer.

Throughout Europe representatives of different religious groups worked to ease the hardships of those who were suffering as a result of the war. The Catholic Church did its part by providing aid for the wounded, the homeless, and prisoners of war in Austria and Germany, as well as in France, Italy, and Belgium. The Lutheran and Calvinist pastors frequently interceded to secure the right to visit prisoner of war camps in France.

Several times the pope attempted to negotiate peace but he was unsuccessful. The governments were involved in a war that would not tolerate the slightest weakness, and which forced the governments to keep on fighting until victory was achieved. Articles in the Vatican newspaper were censored in France as well as Germany, whenever they stated that the pope was discouraging the soldiers. Despite its power and influence, religion could not do anything to put an end to the war.

During a lull in the fighting, a chaplain says a mass outide, on an artillery ammunition wagon. An alert would sometimes interrupt religious services and send everyone hurrying back to their guns.

44

atima, in Portugal, three young shepherds said that they saw Blessed Virgin appear. Great crowds gathered in Portugal. On ober 17, 1917, 70,000 people saw the sun spin around and descend toward the earth. The village became a sanctuary, a center for pilgrimages, where people asked God to bless the soldiers.

rried families who had relatives at the front were exploited by readers, prophets, and fortune-tellers, who claimed they could the future in the cards, and gave good luck charms to the iers for protection. Numerous predictions were sent through mail.

The churches were filled with relics. The faithful rediscovered old observances and practices from the Middle Ages. Candles were lit for patron saints. Saint Radegonde was sought out specifically. She was supposed to protect soldiers in the trenches.

an socialists wouldn't abandon their traditions, even during time. Agrarian socialism was especially deep-rooted on the Pô n, in the north, blending in very well with religion. In the Lom-

bardy villages, peasants were buried with red flags. It was a way of protesting against the war.

Family Life: The Dark Years

Families feared for their loved ones every time a letter was received from the front. Mail was the only connection between the soldiers and their homes. Relatives lived in fear of the day they would receive one of those infamous telegrams from the military announcing the death of a son, husband, or brother. Mail from the survivors at the front was opened with heavy hearts. Each person tried to locate the battlefields of the mobilized soldiers on a war map. But postal censorship was watchful and didn't allow precise details to get through. When there were major battles and offensives, and no letters arrived from the battle zones, every newspaper item was read.

Families, especially large ones, paid a dear price to the war effort by sending the best among them to the front, that is, the strongest of their men. Before the war ended almost all of these families would suffer some sort of loss of someone—to death, as missing in action, wounded, or as prisoners of war. From one day to the next, women became widows and had to find some way to provide for their own needs and those of their families. They were forced to go to work, save and budget, because the war pensions they received were not enough to live on.

Everyday conditions, especially in the cities, were very difficult. The health of adolescents was threatened. About 133,000 children under the age of 18 years old were working in France, and their nutritional condition was unsatisfactory.

Everyone settled down to a precarious existence, waiting for the day to come when the hostilities would come to an end. Fuel and sugar were very scarce. It became harder and harder to get coal, bread, or meat. People made do with what they had by cutting corners. Chickens and geese were raised in the cities. Even in Paris, kitchen gardens were planted in the smallest nooks—on balconies, in courtyards, or on rooftops. Everywhere people had to use their imagination, each day, to make life a little less difficult.

A family reads a letter from the front out loud.

…ermany, even the smallest fragments of cultivatable land were …l. Wheat was planted and potatoes were harvested on the …s of large Bavarian castles. At all costs the undernourished …lation had to be fed.

Wet nurses looked after the undernourished babies of factory workers in Duisbourg and Dusseldorf. They could not be kept in urban homes. Their mothers worked all day long and food was scarce. Milk allotments received from Holland were not enough.

…ance, soup kitchens for primary and nursery school children … set up in many villages. Food was distributed for free. When …women were working in the fields they relied on the aid or-…zed by the schools.

In Germany, there was a lack of teachers. Old retired teachers were called back to their classrooms. The men who were once teachers were now at the front training young recruits between 18 and 19 years old.

…ont of the monuments built in every village, memorial cere-…ies for the war dead were held. A child answered "here" when …ame of someone who died in action was called. The names

of the fallen heroes were lettered on placards with black borders as a sign of mourning.

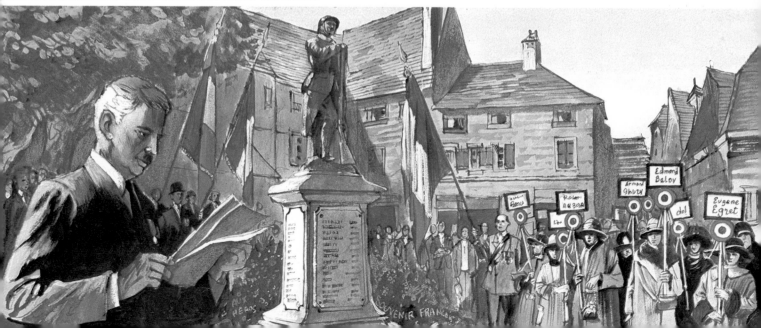

Pleasures at the Rear

The European nations were overwhelmed by a war that had lasted much too long. Populations were displaced and millions of soldiers and workers transported far from their homes. In London, Paris, Bordeaux, and Rouen, soldiers in transit, soldiers on leave, the wounded, factory workers, and foreigners produced varied crowds, which revolutionized everyday life in the cities in the rear.

Paris offered astonishing spectacles. There were workers from everywhere: Indo-Chinese worked in ammunition factories; Algerians, Moroccans, and Martiniquais worked in gas factories. There were also Madagascans and Guiana convicts, repatriated to work under heavy guard, as manual laborers, in work camps outside the city. At the sidewalk cafes you could see Allied soldiers from all over the world—New-Zealanders and Australians, and also by 1918, black Americans.

The men on leave wanted distractions, and in the rear a kind of night life was organized which benefited "goldbricks" and "profiteers" as well who had contracted to work in offices in the rear instead of going to the front. Naturally they were hated by soldiers on leave who stood in line at ticket office windows to get their tickets punched to go back to the front.

The soldiers were annoyed to see that life went on in the rear. The best restaurants were making fortunes and the cafes-concert hadn't closed their doors. Far from the crowded neighborhoods, the "nouveaux rich" showed off their luxuries.

The Americans introduced new jazz rhythms which the Londoners and Parisians were dancing to in a scandalous frenzy of pleasure. It is true that the next day the same dancers very often found themselves in poorly lit trains traveling at twenty miles per hour to be sent to the front as reinforcements. In 1917, Europe was dancing on a volcano about to erupt.

From the Café des Arts to the Café de la Paix, fighting men found each other at the sidewalk cafés of Paris which were never empty. Portuguese and Canadians sat side by side with tanned Legionnaries and Zouaves.

war didn't stop fashion from changing. Dresses were shorter, [mor]e supple and lighter, hats were not as bulky. Women in Berlin [as w]ell as in Paris continued to wear stylish ensembles and buttoned boots, and to carry parasols of fine fabrics. Germany prohibited the selling of silk, it was reserved for use in parachutes.

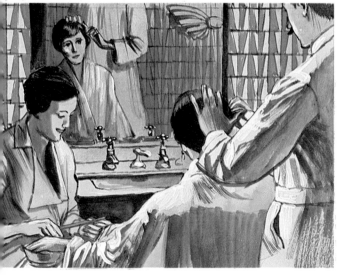

[busi]ness was booming. Women cut their hair short to the dis[plea]sure of the men at the front. Factory workers, office clerks, and [nurs]es in the many hospitals in the rear found this style more [prac]tical.

The new dances were a hit. Besides the tango, everyone was dancing the American one-step, or the fox trot, to jazz music played by black musicians. In 1918, the Yankees (the name for American soldiers) imposed their rhythms on everyone.

[Ma]ny opened ordinary restaurants to feed everyone. However, [the] dishes at regulated prices didn't interest the rich, who had made their fortunes in war industries and now feasted immodestly in the fashionable restaurants of Berlin.

Spies and Saboteurs

The police at the borders were always on the alert, because as the war went on there were an increasing number of spies as the espionage network became well-organized. Undercover agents from other countries entered France from Switzerland, Spain, or Denmark to collect and transmit important information on troop locations, the construction of new weapons, and the preparation of offensives.

The British Intelligence Service was very active in Belgium, where many undercover agents were mixed in with the civilian population. The same was true in Denmark, where the British embassy was a hub of information. The French and the Russians also had very efficient services. France's intelligence department forecast the movement of enemy troops and the direction offensives would take. They gathered a great amount of information from people living in the occupied zone of Alsace-Lorraine and from the French in other invaded departments.

Counterespionage was very active all over Eu-

rope. Barely disembarked, the Americans quickly realized they had to organize a security service among their own troops to prevent infiltration of their units by German spies, recruited in America from among their own mobilized men. The British dispatched spies to the other side of the front by plane. His Majesty's spies had a variety of assignments including missions to collect information or sabotage the railways.

Secret agents who were caught and arrested were treated severely by military justice. After being found guilty, they were quickly shot. Women also participated in espionage activities and were condemned to death exactly as the men were. Mati Hari was executed by the French. The Germans captured the Belgian Martha MacKenna who worked for the British Intelligence Service.

Near the Spanish border, these French police have succeeded in stopping a German agent from escaping to Barcelona. Spain was one of the most active centers in Europe for exchanging intelligence information.

...ary information was transmitted over the radio by Morse code. ...omatic offices in Berne, Switzerland, worked for the espionage ...ices who communicated nonstop with military headquarters ...e belligerent countries.

...arsaw, in 1914, the Russian police were afraid of spies and ...ers, because the Polish, influenced by German propaganda, ...e hostile to the Czarist regime. These Russian soldiers have ...sted a suspicious civilian, and are searching him.

...spy is going to be shot in the moat of the Vincennes castle. ...ead has been hidden with a hood. The French justice system ...not even know his real identity. The head of the Secret Service ...e only one who knows who the spy is.

German deserters escaped via the Belgian-Holland frontier. They crawled through barrels under electric wires. Like these spies, Allied prisoners escaped from prison camps using the same escape plan.

The Germans printed a propaganda newspaper that was distributed throughout the French departments which they occupied. The French secretly printed their own pamphlets that were distributed by hand to inform citizens about the real state of the war.

From War to Revolution

The repeated military defeats and the decline of war, the increase in deprivations and sacrifices supported by the civilian population brought about great exasperation in the rear.

In Dublin in 1916, the Irish revolted against English domination. Beginning in 1917, worker and union movements all over Europe spoke out against a war of annexations and conquests. In Germany the Spartacus League (revolutionary socialists of the far-left) instigated several major social conflicts. As in Germany, there were also violent strikes in France and in Italy.

In Russia, the Revolution of March, 1917, swept the Czarist regime away. But the socialists, with Kerensky as their leader, continued to support the war and planned one last offensive that failed. Lenin and his Bolshevik followers made peace at Brest-Litovsk and disarmed the Czarist army. Along with Trotsky they formed the Red Army to fight against the counterrevolutionary troops. When peace came in 1919, the fate of Russia was still not settled. The fighting continue there between the Red Army and the White troops wh had the support of the West.

Even with peace restored, Europe was to witne several unsettling years of revolutionary and antim litaristic movements brought about by the econom crisis and very low postwar morale. For some peop these revolutionary movements foretold of a sociali Europe that should never fight another war. Since tl autumn of 1918, Germany had experienced a succe sion of insurrections that led to a civil war at the sta of 1919. In Great Britain, the trade unions organize huge strikes in the spring of 1919. In April and Ma of the same year, strikes spread throughout France ar Italy.

After the February-March, 1917 revolution, the majority of worke still did not support the Bolsheviks. Lenin made a tour of factori (here he is at the Paulilov shops) to explain the motives of tl socialist revolution. He expounded the themes of immediate pea and division of land among the peasants.

52

er, 1916, in Dublin Irish nationalists of *Sinn Fein* set off a revolt proclaimed independence for the Irish Republic to fight against militiamen. The British dispatched troops brought in hastily several overseas divisions.

demobilization, Russian soldiers who favored the Bolsheviks ed the Red Army. Their goal was to restore and defend the et Republic against the counterrevolutionaries recruited by the 's army officers and supported militarily by the Allies.

war in Germany. Before the Berlin house of Rudolph-Mosse, r of *Berliner Tageblatt*, a group of revolutionaries, members e Spartacus League, defend a barricade made of large news-r spools topped by unsold bundles. It was January, 1919, and

At the end of the war, dockworkers at Brest demanded higher wages and protested against the hiring of foreign workers. Violent fights broke out on the docks, between the strikers and non-strikers.

the German army had received full power to crush the leftist work-ers' insurrection. The Berlin commune fell after a week of merciless guerrilla warfare.

The Roaring Twenties

Naturally, a sense of great relief was felt at the end of the war. Everyone was exhilarated. After all the suffering, people just wanted to take advantage of life. Women cut their hair and wore short skirts or pants. Most scandalous of all, they began to smoke in public. In France, following the latest trend from America, they began dancing the Charleston to the sound of a saxophone. These happy days at Montparnasse in Paris were famous world wide. The best known artists met and passed many hours at the most fashionable cafes. Balls, shows, horseraces, and seaside-resorts were also part of the scene. The new technologies and industries and the spectacular progress in medical knowledge which were results of the war radically changed people's everyday lives.

Underneath this joyful living, however, people had come to a harsh realization, Europe was no longer the center of the world. The United States had taken its place. The amount of American wealth was incredible. It had allowed the prolongation of the war which, without American money, supplies, and raw material, would never have finished in the Allies favor. Farmers in the midwest and cotton merchants in the south had all made fantastic profits. The New World millionaires went to Europe to spend their newly earned dollars bringing their own fashions with them.

The European governments were ruined. French investors lost everything in Russia, the British insurers suffered great losses as a result of the submarine war. The franc and the pound had been devalued, the mark wasn't worth anything, and inflation was galloping ahead at a rate which prevented the Germans from paying their war debts.

Dancing the Charleston. In Montparnasse dance halls, new dances brought over from the United States grew in popularity.

In January, 1920, the use of alcohol was prohibited in America. During the hours preceding the start of this new law, happy party-goers organized spectacular "funerals of whiskey." Here they dance around a huge bottle of alcohol surrounded by flowers.

Alsace and Lorraine were reattached to France, and Trent, to Italy. Tourist agencies organized trips to become better acquainted with these transitional areas.

Spas became fashionable. Vichy and Plombières, in France, Carlsbad and Baden-Baden in Germany were packed in the summer. Seaside-resorts were also starting to become increasingly popular.

For six days "Winter cycling" was followed under this massive bicycle race-track tent by a varied clientele. Elegant diners mix with the average spectator in the bleachers to watch the riders. In 1921, no stylish Parisian could afford to miss it.

Weekend trains headed for Deauville were being used more and more. Europe was returning to a carefree life style.

A Dairy of the War

by Patrick Restellini

1914, Europe at War

An engraving of the Archduke Franz-Ferdinand's assassination at Sarajevo, June 28, 1914. With this event the war began.

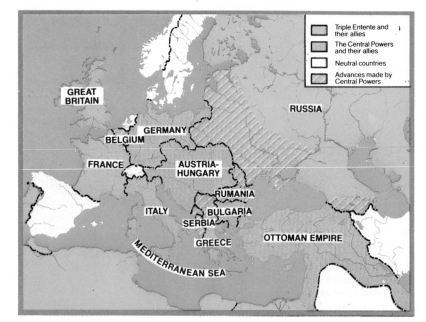

A map of the opposing forces and of maximum territory gained by the Central Powers before its defeat.

June, 1914, An Armed Peace

Europe is now at peace. No one believes that there will be a war. However, the situation is at the mercy of the smallest incident. The match that sets the fire off is the assassination at Sarajevo of the Archduke, heir to the Austrian-Hungarian throne, by a Serbian nationalist (June 28). Backed by Germany, Austria declares war on Serbia, which starts a chain reaction (July 28), that no one can control. Russia (July 30), Germany (August 3), Great Britain (August 4) enter into the war. Turkey joins the side of the Central Powers (Germany-Austria) November 29. Italy is the only one that stays neutral.

A huge wave of nationalism overwhelms Europe. No one can stop it. Jaurés, a socialist, who symbolizes the power of peace, is assassinated (July 31).

The War Movement

All over Europe, the armies are marching to the borders. The Germans implement the Schlieffen plan. Planned since 1900, they concentrate a huge attack on the French forces, while Austria-Hungary holds off the Russian army in the East.

August 4, 1914
Belgium invaded

While the French are amassing their army in Lorraine, Germany is invading Belgium, a neutral country, throwing several divisions on the northern front.

August 23, 1914

After being driven from the field at Charleroi, the French beat a retreat before the Germans, who will soon threaten Paris.

August 26–31, 1914
The Battle of Tannenberg

The Russians have taken the initiative on the Eastern front, making the Germans evacuate East Prussia. Hindenberg stops them at the Battle of Tannenberg (Poland, formerly East Prussia). 100,000 Russians are taken prisoner.

September 6–12, 1914
The first Battle of the Marne

Taking advantage of a German error, the French counterattack under the leadership of Gallieni and Joffre, and force the Germans to withdraw toward the northwest to avoid being surrounded.

The Belgian king and his military staff working in the trenches.

September 7, 1914

The Russians are defeated at the Mazuries lakes. In Galicia, the Austrians lose at Lemberg.

October 10–November 10, 1914
The Sea Race

Incapable of winning a decisive battle, one million Allied troops and one million Germans try to outflank each other in the West. A succession of battles push the front lines toward the North Sea. The battles end after a German loss on the Yser and Ypres rivers. Henceforth, the Western front becomes fixed on a line reaching from Belgium to the Swiss border. Open field warfare takes the place of a warfare based on positions. The soldiers are stuck in the trenches, they watch carefully before attacking under shell and machine-gun fire. The war will last three years and more than three million will die.

November 2, 1914

Great Britain proclaims the North Sea a war zone, thus reinforcing the blockade of the Central Powers.

French soldiers equipped with rudimentary gas masks and metal helmets.

Trench Warfare
February 5, 1915

In response to the blockade of its coasts, Germany announces a blockade of the Allied Powers' coasts and orders its submarines to attack all cargo ships, even neutral ones. The war is spreading throughout the oceans.

February 16–March 10, 1915
The French offensive in Champagne

All of Joffre's efforts are directed at a breakthrough on the front, no matter what the cost or the amount of suffering for the fighting men. The losses are heavy (almost 100,000 dead) and the results are negligible.

A Naval battle in the Straits of the Dardanelles.

February 18–April 19, 1915
The Dardanelles expedition against the Turks

A French-British defeat. On the other hand the Turks unsuccessfully attack the Suez canal which is defended by the British and the Persians.

April, 1915

With the support of Austria-Hungary, the Germans attack on the Eastern front. The Russian defenses are penetrated.

April 22, 1915
The Battle of Ypres

For the first time, the Germans use asphyxiating gasses. Twenty out of every hundred soldiers fighting on the front are affected, one quarter of them are killed. New weapons make their appearance: grenades and trench howitzers. In the meantime aviation is starting to be used to direct artillery fire, photograph enemy positions, and bomb the rear.

May 9–June 18, 1915

An Allied offensive in Artois. The French lose more than 100,000 men.

May 7, 1915

The British liner, the *Lusitania*, is torpedoed and sunk by a German submarine. (There are 1,200 victims, 118 of whom are Americans). The United States protests, causing the Germans to limit further actions of this sort.

May 23, 1915

Italy joins the Allied side in the war, opening a new front in the south of Europe. They suffer a defeat in the Alps at the hands of Austria-Hungary.

Czar Nicholas II at the head of his troops.

June-July 1915

The Russians lose Galicia, Lithuania, and Poland to Germany and Austria-Hungary.

June 3, 1915

The Turkish government decides to exterminate Armenians suspected of supporting the Russians (one and half million are killed).

September-October, 1915

French offensive in Champagne (150,000 killed). Bulgaria joins the Central Powers in the war, causing Serbia's collapse. The Allies cannot help them, because they are cut off at Salonika.

A war scene in the trenches: Russian soldiers are equipped French style.

September 5, 1915

Socialist meeting at Zimmerwald in Switzerland is called by the Russian leader Lenin. It is the first time, since the beginning of the war, that socialist groups from the two sides meet.

November 13, 1915
The Eastern Front

Russia invades Prussia and Armenia. The British advance toward Baghdad.

January, 1916

The Spartacus League, a revolutionary socialist and pacifist group, is founded in Germany.

February 21–July, 1916
The Battle of Verdun

The German military staff's goal is to bleed the French army to death, obliging them to use all their reserves. Petain, who was called to command the troops at Verdun, proclaims "They will not get past us." The forts of Hill 304, Douaumont, Vaux, and the Mort-Homme are taken and retaken in bloody battles. From March to December, an average of 150,000 to 200,000 shells are fired daily. After very heavy losses (600,000 are killed in all), Verdun remains in French hands.

A giant 420 mm unexploded German shell

April 24, 1916

Easter Monday, Irish nationalists revolt in Dublin.

May 31, 1916
The Naval Battle of Jutland

The Germans lose three cruisers, six torpedo boats, and three battleships while the British lose five cruisers, and one battleship. The German fleet reaches its bases, where it will stay until the end of the war. The British are now masters of the seas.

June, 1916

The Russian General Broussilov's first offensive in Galicia. The Austrians are pushed back as far as the Carpathians.

July 1–November 12, 1916
The Somme offensive

The Allies, who are well equipped (flamethrowers, grenade launchers, machine guns, mortars and 37 mm guns), win a few battles. The British use their tanks for the first time, without success (615,000 Allies are killed, 420,000 of them are British; 650,000 Germans are killed).

August 29, 1916

Rumania enters the war on the Allied side.

November 24, 1916

Greece enters the war against Bulgaria and Germany.

December, 1916

The uselessness of the heavy sacrifices reported by all the belligerents produce a pacifist movement and agitation among workers in France as well as in Germany. In Russia the situation is critical. Supplies don't arrive in the cities, prices rise, the people are tired of the war and of making sacrifices, the army is exhausted and demoralized after the defeat of the Broussilov offensive. Strikes take place in the major industrial centers.

The German Lieutenant Rackow: he was the first one to enter the fort of Vaux at Verdun.

A battle scene at Verdun: the German infantry attacks

April 16, 1917

The Nivelle offensive at *Chemin des Dames*. A bloody defeat. The French lose 271,000 men in just ten days of fighting.

May, 1917
Mutiny in the French army

Petain, who was named commander-in-chief, reacts firmly. A total of 400 men are sentenced to be court martialed, 45 of them will be executed. At the same time, Petain improves the soldiers' living conditions and decides to wait for tanks and the Americans before taking up the offensive again.

In Germany, there are strikes in the armaments industry and mutinies in the navy. The population is unhappy about difficulties obtaining food.

A group of American officers on a battlefield in 1917

The President of the United States, Woodrow Wilson

October, 1917

The Italians lose at Caporetto at the hands of Austria-Hungary. The Italian army retreats to the Piave River, leaving 300,000 prisoners and half of its artillery behind.

November 6–7, 1917

Lenin and the Bolsheviks seize power at Petrograd. They start negotiations with the Central Powers to end any Russian obligations toward the war.

November 17, 1917

Constitution of Prime Minister Clemenceau who begins an energetic campaign against defeatism and proclaims his firm intention to stay in the war until it is won.

December 12–30, 1916

After its victory over occupied Rumania, Germany proposes peace to the Allies, with the United States acting as an intermediary. The Allies refuse the German overtures which they find outrageous.

The Decisive Year

January 28, 1917

Germany decides to start the submarine war again. During 1917 ships weighing a total of five million tons are sunk. The French armaments factories go on strike.

March 8, 1917
The Russian Revolution

Czar Nicholas II abdicates on March 15. The temporary government, nevertheless, asserts its faithfulness to Russia's "international responsibilities."

April 6, 1917

The United States enters the war after two American vessels are torpedoed. The Allies benefit from the boundless credits that will finance their war efforts. Two months later, the first American contingent will set foot on French soil (by the end of 1917, there will be 250,000 American soldiers).

November 26, 1917

Russian Soviets ask for an armistice.

December, 1917

The British encourage the Arabs to revolt against the Turks and take possession of Jerusalem and Baghdad.

Allied Victory

January 8, 1918

President Wilson's 18 Points Plan: renunciation of secret diplomacy, freedom of the seas, the right of people to self-determination, the return of Alsace-Lorraine to France, the creation of a League of Nations.

March 3, 1918
The Brest-Litovsk treaty

Thr Russians sign a peace treaty, stating that Germany will have Poland, the Baltic countries, and the Ukraine's natural resources (Ukrainia is to become an independent republic). With the end of the war in the East, Germany sends all of its forces to the West.

March 21, 1918

The Ludendorff offensive in Picardie. The Germans advance thirty-eight miles in one week, but they are finally stopped.

A photographic mission is being prepared.

April, 1918

The Ludendorff offensive in Flanders. The British are saved at the last minute, by the French.

May 27, 1918

The German offensive in Champagne, at Chemin des Dames. The Germans are only forty-four miles from Paris. "Big Bertha" shells the capital for the first time.

July 18, 1918

Under Foch's orders the Allies, numerically stronger (211 divisions, 104 of which are French, to 181 German divisions), counter-attack. This surprises the Germans, who are forced to retreat.

August 8, 1918

Foch's offensive in Picardie. . . . Hundreds of tanks thrown into battle crush the front. The Germans are forced to beat a retreat.

September 15, 1918

The Salonika army, under Franchet d'Esperey's leadership, cracks the Bulgarian front, and frees Serbia and Rumania.

September 16, 1918

Last shelling of Paris.

September 28, 1918

A new Allied offensive, which forces the Germans to retreat from the North Sea to the Meuse River.

September 29, 1918

The top German military staff asks Kaiser Wilhelm II to open negotiations with the Allies for an armistice.

Surrounded by German soldiers, French war prisoners
finish peeling potatoes.

October 24, 1918

Vittorio Venetto's Italian victory. The Austrian-Hungarians are defeated.

October 30, 1918

Turkey surrenders—the Moudros Armistice.

November 3, 1918

Revolts break out in the German fleet at Kiel and in several large cities at the announcement of a request for an armistice.

November 4, 1918

Italian-Austrian Armistice. A few days earlier, the Austrian-Hungarian Empire had been divided: Czechoslovakia and Hungary have seceded; Yugoslavia has been created.

November 9, 1918

Kaiser Wilhelm II abdicates. The socialist Schneidemann proclaims a republic in Germany.

November 11, 1918
The signing of the Armistice at Rethondes

The war is over; losses are heavy on both sides. Germany—1.9 million dead; Russia—1.7 million; France—1.4 million; Austria-Hungary—1 million; Great Britain—935,000; Italy—496,000; Serbia—400,000; Turkey—400,000; Rumania—250,000; the United States—115,000. Almost 9 million in all.

January 18, 1919

The Peace Conference opens at Versailles. Discussions among the Italian Orlando, the British Lloyd George, the French Clemenceau, and the American Wilson. The losers are not present at the conference.

June 28, 1919

The Versailles Treaty, the final and official end to the war, imposes tough conditions on the losers. Germany must give Alsace-Lorraine back to France and must pay heavy reparations to the Allies.

September 10, 1919

The Treaty of Saint Germain-en-Laye with Austria-Hungary. Austria-Hungary is broken up and reduced to just Austria. Czechoslovakia, Hungary, Poland, and Yugoslavia become independent nations.

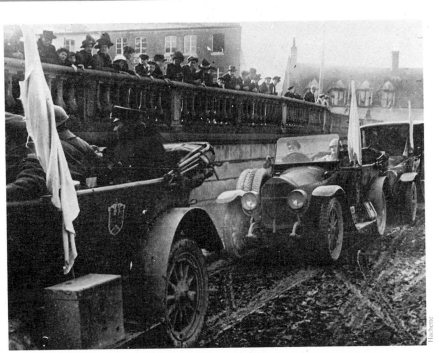

Members of the German Parliament arrive with a white flag to sign the armistice.

An engraving shows the signing of the armistice on November 11, 1918.

Glossary

Allied Powers The countries who fought against Germany and Austria-Hungary in World War I.
Allies Countries who are united with each other during a war.
Armament The act of preparing for war.
Armistice An official, but temporary end to fighting in a war.
Arsenal A place where military weapons are stored, manufactured, or repaired.
Artillery The large-caliber cannons and mounted guns used by the army.
Autocrat A ruler who has absolute power over his subjects.

Bolsheviks The radical political party in Russia that seized power from the czar in 1917.
Bombard To drop bombs on or to attack heavily with fire from artillery.

Casualty A member of the military who has been killed, captured, or injured in the war.
Censorship The practice of deleting information from communications (letters or newspapers) that may be harmful if it was to become general knowledge or fall into the wrong hands.
Central Powers Germany and Austria-Hungary and the countries allied with them in World War I.
Counterattack An attack made in return of an enemy's attack.
Counterespionage Espionage directed at confusing or preventing enemy espionage.

Deserter A member of the military who, without permission, runs away from duty.
Dreadnought A large battleship armed with big guns.

Epidemic An outbreak of a disease that spreads very quickly and affects many people at one time.
Espionage Spying to collect military secrets.

Fraternization To associate with enemy soldiers.
Front A line of battle.

Infantry Soldiers who have been trained and equipped to fight on foot.

Jerry A German soldier.

Kaiser The title given to the emperor of Germany from 1871-1918.

Maim To suffer a serious physical injury that causes permanent damage.
Matériel All the supplies and equipment used by an army.
Mobilize To call troops together and prepare them for war.
Mortar A short cannon that fires shells at a high angle so they drop on their target from above.
Mutiny A rebellion by military personnel against their officers.

Neutral To take no side in a war.

Offensive An attack.

Pacifist Someone who is against war and believes that peaceful methods should be used to end or solve conflicts.
Propaganda Information spread to improve one's own position or undermine the enemy's position.

Rear The area farthest from the enemy.
Refugee A person who has fled from their own country during a war.

Sabotage Damage done to slow down the enemy's war effort.
Sapper A soldier who works at building trenches and other fortifications.

Yankees Nickname for soldiers from the United States.

INDEX